By sharing her tr........ ......g a child and later fin...... .....kin had been retained, Debbie ......kin hopes it may bring comfort to others who have suffered a painful loss. She also hopes it will raise professional awareness, allowing insight into the personal impact of such a loss.

Debbie Ruskin was born in Birmingham. She is married, with 4 children and now lives in Manchester. Still a Brummie at heart, she is a keen supporter of Birmingham City football club.

Debbie is a university graduate and a qualified counsellor. While her children were young, she was an active member of the National Childbirth Trust, being a local branch leader for 5 years. She now works for a number of counselling organisations, both in a paid and voluntary capacity.

If this story helps or touches another human soul, then Lisa's short life has some meaning, that although she could not live herself, the spirit of her flame will continue to glow.

A Candle for Lisa

Debbie Ruskin

Pennine Pens

Published 2002 by Pennine Pens
Copyright © the author
All rights reserved

ISBN 1 873378 78 5

Typeset and published by Pennine Pens.
32, Windsor Road, Hebden Bridge,
West Yorkshire, HX7 8LF.
Tel 01422-843724
Fax 01422-847369
books@penpens.demon.co.uk
http://www.hebdenbridge.co.uk
http://www.penninepens.co.uk

~ PROLOGUE ~

This is the story of a candle whose little flame only flickered for a short while before it was snuffed out. A story of a little girl called Lisa who was not given the chance to live.

Lisa was my little girl. So this is also a story about myself - about how it feels to lose a child and to carry on living with that loss, knowing that maybe she could have been given the chance to live.

It is going to be a difficult story to write, difficult to confront all the pain and then expose it for others to read. Yet, I feel this is a story that needs to be told.

I know that telling my story will not bring back my little girl. Nor will trying to apportion blame. But I am left with questions unanswered. Did the hospital staff give her the chance she deserved? Why was I put in the position I was, to be left to live with the consequences? I would like to hope that by writing this, maybe hospitals will learn from my story. Then Lisa will not have died in vain.

It is also my hope, that by sharing my painful experiences, I may bring some comfort to others who have suffered the loss of a child. A loss that many people do not want to think about, let alone hear us talk about. A loss that unless you have been there yourself, is just too unimaginable to really understand.

Maybe writing this will help me to live with what has happened. And maybe, just maybe, salvage some treasure from the wreckage of pain, that is a gift for the future.

If this story touches any human soul then I will feel that Lisa's short life has some meaning, that although she could not live herself, the spirit of her flame will continue to glimmer on....

~ *Chapter One* ~

ANTICIPATION

I begin this story with hope. It is the hope that comes with expecting a baby. The word 'expecting' conjures up the feelings of excitement and anticipation, waiting to welcome into the world a new little life and the potential that a new life can promise.

My life seemed almost perfect. Small things had gone wrong from time to time, as they do, but I just regarded them as nuisances. Tragic events happened to other people. It never occurred to me that they could descend on us.

I was in my mid-twenties. I had a close-knit family, lots of friends and a happy marriage. Stephen and I already had a little girl, Claire, who was just over a year old when we found out that I was expecting another child. We envisaged a second child would make what was perfect, even better.

This pregnancy was good, although not quite as good as my first one. I am a small person and carried 'light', hardly ever feeling sick or in discomfort. I just felt a bit weird and 'not myself'. I knew that each pregnancy could be different and put this feeling down to being pregnant, believing that I would feel like myself again once the baby was born.

I felt special being pregnant, knowing that I was carrying a developing new life inside me. A unique and wonderful experience that only a woman can have.

I looked forward to giving Claire a brother or sister and liked the idea that they would be close in age. Idealistically, I was hoping it would follow that they would also be close as siblings. I enjoyed what I considered to be the important honour of choosing a name for this new little person. I had a sense that the baby would be a girl but we had a name ready for a boy or a girl. As the seasons changed and my stomach slowly grew bigger, I contentedly imagined what life would be like with two little children.

We started preparing for the new baby. We created a nursery by clearing the junk from what we had called the spare bedroom. We had most of the baby equipment already from having Claire. We just needed a double buggy. We had selected one but, so as not to tempt fate, we would not buy it until after the birth. We only bought some first size nappies, which would be needed straight away. I found all the baby clothes that Claire had once worn. They looked so tiny. I picked up a little babygrow and imagined the new baby wearing it.

A late ultrasound scan revealed the sex of the baby. Although I only had a few weeks to wait till the baby would be born, we liked the idea of knowing what the baby would be. We found out we were having a little girl, as I had thought. She would be a sister for Claire. From then on she was no longer 'the Bump' or 'the Baby' – she was Lisa.

It was now Spring, yet the air still had a biting winter's chill. I was 32 weeks pregnant. A strong feeling came over me that Lisa would be born in two weeks time. In fact, it was more than a feeling. I had a sense of certainty that by the Wednesday in two weeks time my baby would be here.

Stephen's reaction to my announcement was a bemused 'I see'. The hospital midwife who saw me at my next antenatal appointment was stonily unconvinced. Hardly surprising really. She seemed as cold as the poky room we were in. She said there was no reason to suggest that my baby would arrive early and, anyway, she would be more likely to know than I was. My sense of conviction was squashed.

We were going to spend a week with my parents, who still lived in my hometown, 40 miles from where we lived. I always enjoyed going 'home'. My parents had moved to a flat and no longer lived in the house in which I grew up. However, there was a comfortable familiarity in going back to visit them and seeing family and childhood friends. Sometimes my brother and sister-in-law also visited at the same time, but this time they could not get the time off work.

On the Monday we strapped Claire into the

baby seat in the back of the car and loaded all the bags. With all the stuff for a toddler, it looked like we were going to stay for a month. As we set off, I was aware that this would probably be the last opportunity to visit my parents before the baby was born. I was 34 weeks pregnant and travelling would soon be unwise.

A relaxing week stretched out ahead of us. My larger shape was making me slower. It was a time to take it easy and be looked after by my parents for a while. It would give me a welcome break from doing the 'looking after'.

I had a huge sense of contentment watching how much pleasure my parents got from little Claire. With her ginger curls and continual smile, she was now a delightful 21 months old. She was their first grandchild and next time we visited we would be bringing their second grandchild too. I was looking forward to what the future would deliver.

~ *Chapter 2* ~

A NIGHTMARE BEGINS

In an idyllic place sometimes, unknown to anyone, trouble bubbles ominously below the surface, waiting to erupt and shatter the lives of those around.

It was now Wednesday. Unaware of the date or its earlier significance, our visit to my parents had to come to an abrupt end.

I awoke to find that I had lost some blood. It seemed quite a lot. I knew that losing any blood is worrying in pregnancy and I wanted the reassurance of being checked out at the local maternity hospital. We dressed and my Dad drove Stephen and me the short distance to the hospital, whilst Mum looked after Claire.

It was strange having to make an unscheduled visit to a different hospital, which had not monitored my pregnancy nor had my pregnancy records. However, Claire was born at this hospital shortly before moving towns. Although they did not have my current notes, they did still have the notes from my first pregnancy. This helped to ease the strangeness and give me a sense of familiarity and calm.

The admissions area of the delivery suite had a high ceiling and a row of curtained-off beds. We were led to one bed and the curtain was drawn round us. The curtain only offered privacy from view. We could hear the conversations and periodic groans from the next occupied bed. After a while I could hear them being transferred to a delivery room and later someone else arriving and taking that bed.

We were there for two or three hours while the midwife checked me over. Monitors were attached to check the baby. She could not pick up Lisa's heartbeat on the machine, but she could hear it with the funny 'trumpet' that she pressed on my stomach. I was a little bit unsettled but the midwife reassured me that these things can happen and that the baby was fine.

I was fine too. My cervix was 'hard' which meant that I was not in labour, nor was I about to go into labour. We were advised it would be best to travel back home the same day, although we could have lunch first, as there was really no rush. I did not need to call in at my usual hospital until my next antenatal appointment the following week. Again I was told that everything was all right.

I don't remember lunch at all, except that Mum had put out food that she knew we liked to eat. I made sure that Claire ate something before travelling back. But I felt edgy and unable to eat, as I was anxious to leave.

Soon Stephen had all the bags loaded into the car, Claire was strapped in and Mum and Dad waved us off from the entrance to the flats. They continued to wave as they always did until we were out of sight.

I was driving, because Stephen had not yet learnt to drive. My enlarged stomach was almost touching the steering wheel. As we progressed through the fairly light afternoon traffic, I began to relax.

We drove through the city centre and picked up the road heading north to where we lived. After a while we came to the large roundabout on the outskirts, beyond which the road becomes an open carriageway leaving the city behind. And, as we approached the roundabout, I went into labour.

I tried to stay calm. We still had a choice. We could turn round at the roundabout and head back through the city to the maternity hospital that I had just been to earlier. Or we could continue on home and go to the hospital there.

Turning back would mean travelling about ten miles, but it would be through the city and all its traffic, traffic lights and other obstacles. Continuing on meant travelling another 35 miles, but at least it would be on the 'open' road and the hospital was visible on the approach into the town. We both instantaneously felt that this would be the better option.

The road is normally busy and this afternoon was no exception. Stephen wished that he could drive. It had never been important to him before, as we lived on a good bus route and if we travelled out of town then I could drive. But now we were in the middle of nowhere, I was driving and in labour.

I stayed in the slow lane as cars in the faster lanes sped by. The journey back was like a horrendous dream. I felt I was outside of myself, as if it was not really happening to me. Yet I was also acutely aware that it was really happening. I was in labour. Contractions were now coming every 5 minutes and I had to drive, with (including Lisa) four lives in my hands.

Staying in the slow lane allowed me to mount the bank of the road and stop for each contraction. There was no hard shoulder to stop on, as this was not a motorway, only grassy banks which sloped at 45 degrees. Stephen encouraged me to concentrate as hard as I could on driving between my contractions. He would time things and warn me after 4 minutes, so that I could mount the bank for the next imminent contraction. After which, I rejoined the road for another 4 minutes until I had to pull off again. And then pulling off again and again all the way home.

The contractions got stronger but thankfully not more frequent. The 45-minute journey took nearly two hours. As I grew more and more tired and anxious, I tried to imagine Claire and Lisa soon sitting side by side in the back of the car and willed myself to keep going.

At last we were home. I felt completely drained and immobilised. Stephen made me a hot drink, which I sipped in an attempt to recoup some energy. Meanwhile, he phoned for a taxi to take me to hospital.

Stephen could not go with me but would come as soon as he had found a babysitter for Claire. I kissed them both and got into the taxi, exhausted and nervous. Contractions were now intensifying, but I knew I would make it to hospital. Lisa would soon be here.

~ *Chapter 3* ~

A Fleeting Flame

Once in hospital, with the drama of getting there behind me, I was escorted along white-walled corridors to the delivery suite. Without Stephen with me, I felt like a lone warrior facing a long battle without reinforcement.

I was shown into the delivery room. There was a bed and instruments all around. It was bleak and clinical, even though the room had pastel florally wallpaper in an attempt to make it more congenial. It was now about 5 o'clock. Midwives scurried in and out, checking how far labour had progressed and trying to make me comfortable. Not that I had exactly any prospect of being comfortable. But Stephen would soon be here to hold my hand.

Eventually Stephen arrived. Labour was progressing well and I did now feel relatively comfortable with an epidural in place to control the pain. One midwife was more or less continually with me. I began to relax, with the thought that the torture of nature taking its course would not be too bad after all.

Time ticked by. The midwife alternated between monitoring my progress, offering encouraging words and engaging Stephen and me in pleasant light-hearted conversation. Although it seemed incongruous on the approach to welcoming a new life, I appreciated the distraction it offered.

It was now past midnight. The midwife checked the baby again. Suddenly she announced that the baby was in distress. She dashed out and then swiftly came back with another midwife, who also checked and agreed that things were not going right. I needed to have an emergency caesarean section to deliver the baby as quickly as possible.

My hopes that it would at least be done under the epidural that was already in place were abruptly dashed. It would take twenty minutes for the epidural to be topped up sufficiently in order to perform a caesarean. This was an emergency that could not wait that long. It had to be a general anaesthetic and it had to be now.

My mind went into a whirl as the epidural was removed and I was wheeled to theatre in the early hours of Thursday morning. What was happening? Yet I knew what was happening. Would the baby be all right? Would I wake up again after the anaesthetic? I tried to suppress my fear by telling myself that I'd soon come too again - and actually have my baby girl.

At the theatre doors, Stephen was told to go and wait until they came to fetch him. His baby would be born in ten minutes. As these words were being spoken, I was pushed into the operating theatre. The doors closed and the room vaporised as I drifted off.

The next thing I knew was becoming drowsily aware of a woman's voice coming from somewhere around. It was telling me: 'Debbie, you have a little girl…' And then '…I'm sorry she's not very well…' I heard this, but I did not have time to take in the enormity of the situation before drifting back to sleep.

I had no idea of time, but it would have been about two hours later when I became aware of Stephen by my side. I was still just as drowsy but knew he was there. Other people were there too. I was not awake enough to take them in but they were talking to me none the less. A male voice was gently dropping the bombshell.

'Your baby is on a life support machine… She has heart and lung problems… I'm sorry. We've done all we can…' My baby! What are they saying? '… It would be for the best if we switch off the machine... Debbie… we need your permission to turn it off.'

The information sunk in. They wanted to switch off the machine that was keeping my baby alive. They were giving up on her. But they couldn't do that. I wanted my baby. While there is life there is hope. I have always felt this. I tried to tell them. The words went loudly round and round in my head but I was too drowsy to get them out of my mouth.

Inside I was screaming 'No! No!' But could they hear me? It was like one of those bad dreams where I was going to drown unless I managed to get to the water's edge. However hard I tried to swim, nothing seemed to be happening and I was about to go down. I was calling out, but was anybody hearing me? I had to be heard.

It seems that I was heard enough for them to say, 'It is better to let her die with dignity'. That was the blow that pushed me under. I felt as if I was drowning. I was struggling to stay awake and was struggling to think.

They can't do it. I wanted my baby. But keeping her alive would be denying Lisa her dignity. Was my wanting to keep her alive being selfish? How could I deny my little girl her dignity? I felt squashed. I felt as if all the air had gone out of me. I had no more strength left and could no longer refuse.

Still drowsy, I was aware that Lisa's life support machine was being turned off. I felt numb and deflated. Soon Lisa was being carried into the room, wrapped in a small white blanket.

She was first given to Stephen to hold for a while. I saw how tenderly he held our new baby.

Then she was handed to me. I was still lying on the bed, unable to sit up, as I took hold of my child. Wrapped in the blanket, all I could see of her was her head. She had golden ginger curly hair and in her face I could see a sisterly resemblance to Claire. Her eyes were shut and her little mouth was closed in a relaxed sleepy sort of way. She looked so peaceful - and so perfect. Here was a new little life. I could not believe I was being handed my baby for her to die.

Somebody had the foresight to take some photographs of Lisa, which are now such precious and tangible mementoes of her short life.

Still wrapped in the blanket, I held her close to my body as she died in my arms.

~ *Chapter 4* ~

SHATTERED

After Lisa died, Stephen and I were left alone with her for a while. We took turns to hold her. There was a stillness in the room. It felt like we were suspended in time, stunned by the enormity of what had happened.

Then a couple of people came back into the room. I was going to be taken up to the ward. This would mean that Stephen would have to go back home. It was now about 4.30 in the morning and Stephen must have been exhausted. But he would be going back alone and in pieces after his loss, at a time when the rest of the world would be asleep. I was acutely aware that there would be nobody there for him but, still sleepy, I just could not offer him anything myself. The only person he could possibly contact at this unearthly hour was my brother. 'Phone Dan', I urged, hoping that he would be all right.

I was transferred to a side room back on the antenatal ward, away from the new babies. They allowed Lisa to come with me. I remember drifting in and out of sleep with Lisa beside me in the bed. I knew she was dead, but I just could not stay awake to really savour these last moments with her. But I do remember the feel of her lying beside me, the feel of my arm round her little body and every now and again waking sufficiently to hold her close, before drifting off back to sleep.

Lisa was with me for a long time. It was mid-morning when a midwife came into the room and said that it was time they should be taking her away. My Mum was also in the room. She must have travelled up with my Dad when she heard the news. She asked if she could hold Lisa. I'd had about six hours of sleepy togetherness with Lisa and I realised that she could not stay with me forever. I knew it was time to let her go.

Mum gently asked me if I would like it if she carried Lisa down to the morgue. I felt that, as I could not take her myself and Stephen was not here, there was no better person than my Mum to carry her. She would hold Lisa on her passage from the warmth of my bed to the cold, lifeless place she was being taken to. My Mum would carry her lovingly and look after her. The midwife opened the door and with Lisa in Mum's arms they left the room. Alone and empty, I drifted back to sleep.

The rest of that day passed in a haze, alternating between sleep and a numb emptiness. Every now and then, a midwife came in to check on me. At one point she seemed concerned that my blood pressure had dropped extremely low and was returning to check it every 15 minutes. I remember the effort of having to lift my seemingly heavy arm for her yet again.

Stephen came back and later my parents appeared. My brother Dan and sister-in-law Nikki had travelled five hours to come and see me, yet I just could not keep my eyes open for more than five minutes. But I appreciated them all for being there.

The next day was Friday. I propped myself up in the hospital bed and looked around at the plain magnolia walls. I was now more alert and the full impact of my loss began to hit me. It felt like I had been cut open and part of my very being had been ripped out. I had no baby – she was no longer inside me and yet she was not here beside me as I had expected her to be. She had gone. And with the loss, I had lost the future I had envisaged with her – looking after a new baby, toddler-hood, starting school, growing up, having another daughter, a sister for Claire... The loss just seemed too much.

The pain was so overwhelming and pervasive, the aching emptiness and devastation just too intense. The hospital had given me some booklets about losing a baby. It felt unreal and yet at the same time, it was too painful to confront my loss so soon, in black and white. I could not settle. I could not apply my mind to anything, yet could not cope with staying with the pain that was there. I tried playing music over the headphones but it jarred with the turmoil in my head. So I turned it off and then I could not stand the quiet. I could not escape the unbearable intensity of my emotions.

Stephen arrived late morning. My parents were looking after Claire so that he could visit. I knew that only Stephen could understand how I was feeling, as he must have been feeling it too. With his arms round me, the tears just flowed and flowed. We talked and had times of silent togetherness. Stephen revealed that when I was taken into theatre, he had been told that our baby would be born in ten minutes. But no one came back to him for two whole hours. He had been beside himself with worry. They had been trying to stabilise Lisa, but he had feared that something had happened to me. And he was also aching from the loss of our child.

In the evening, I remember him helping me out of bed, which was still painful for me after the surgery. He took me to the window. It was now dark outside and we could see many windows in other wings of the hospital all lit up. It was a very poignant moment. Standing close together, Stephen said, 'look out over there, Debbie, at all those windows. All over the hospital there are babies being born, people who die and medical people trying to save and treat others. Some of them get better and go home and there are some that don't…'

The following morning, a friend called in to see

me. I had been crying when she knocked on the door. I felt embarrassed that she had caught me in this state, despite the fact it was hardly surprising, having just lost my baby two days earlier. I also felt that we were different now – I had suffered a dreadful loss and she had not, and my distress clearly made her feel uncomfortable.

As the news spread, more and more friends came to visit me, some coming from out of town. By now I was composed. I appreciated their coming. Their presence was a welcome distraction and I was relatively cheerful.

Katrina, my longest childhood friend appeared. We were very close although we did not see each other as often now that we lived in different towns. I remember her words as she came and sat down by my bed. 'For the first time in my life, Debbie, I just don't know what to say to you.' It was so touchingly honest and genuine. And with the same honesty I said, 'I don't know what to say to you either, I'm just glad you're here.'

Stephen arrived with the news that Lisa's funeral had been arranged. It would be tomorrow. I was shaken by this news. Having just had a caesarean and the stitches were still in, would I be able to go? Who had arranged it and why so soon?

I had to be there to bury my little girl. A doctor came and asserted that it would not be possible so soon after surgery. The need to be there was so desperate that I insisted I wanted to go. My insistence went almost all the way to the top and the Senior Registrar came to see me. He was not happy for me to go but he understood my need. If I promised to be taken by car, sit for as long as possible until actually at the graveside and then get back into the car and come straight back to hospital, then I could go. I was elated. I had won an 'exit visa' to go to my Lisa's funeral.

Stephen was not so elated. He was upset and worried that my wound might open.

Jack, a close friend of ours, arrived. Stephen told him that I wanted to go to the funeral. Jack was adamant, 'Debbie, you can't do this to Stephen, he's also lost his child you know. You can't add to his grief by making him worry about you as well.'

Again my needs and feelings were squashed. My elation in being able to go had now turned to guilt, that I had not considered how it would affect Stephen. Although I was desperate to go, I now felt that I no longer could. Family and friends would be there to see my little girl laid to rest. But me, her mother, would not be there and that felt really bad.

On the day of the funeral, Stephen had arranged for Claire to go and stay with a friend. My sister-in-law Nikki and a friend Anna came to the hospital to be with me. It helped not to be on my own. At the time the funeral was taking place, they sat in silence with me. I tried to feel something. But I felt absolutely nothing.

Fifteen minutes later it seemed to darken outside and an eerie feeling descended in the room. Nikki and Anna both said they did not notice anything. I later learnt that Lisa's funeral had been delayed by 15 minutes and took comfort from the fact that I had, after all, been with her in spirit.

After five days in hospital, I was well enough to go home. I did not want to go home to the house that was meant to welcome Lisa. Stephen had already done the dismal tasks of taking back the nappies and putting away all the baby clothes. He had returned the room we had ready for Lisa to how it used to be. But I did not want to confront the 'how it used to be' and the empty gap that could not be covered up. I wanted to move house. Then I would not have to live in the house that held shattered dreams.

The Ward Sister called in to see me that morning and I told her how I felt. 'But you can always have another baby later', she said.

Her platitude hit me like a slap in the face. I did not want another baby. I wanted Lisa. I desperately wanted her. It was as if she was denying my loss and my feelings. I was shocked that the Sister, in her senior position could have said such a thing. It was as if, despite all her authority and expertise, she was not able to be there and listen to me in the way I needed.

I knew, in the back of my mind, that moving would only add to the stress I already had. I could not run away from it by moving house, as the pain would only follow me.

My body would not let me escape the pain. I was still sore from the caesarean. My milk was now coming through, but I had no baby to feed, which intensified the loss and emptiness even more.

Dan, who is a doctor, had told me that my pain was like a wound. At first it would be red and raw. Then as it slowly healed it would become less red and less sore and after a while I would not notice it all the time. Then as more time passed, it would form a scar and gradually the scar would fade, but it would never totally disappear. I would carry the memory with me. This really helped. I had been wounded, emotionally, and this gave me some hope that eventually my pain would lessen.

But for now, I would have to go home without my baby, with the intense ache of empty arms . . . and hope I could make it through the days ahead.

~ *Chapter 5* ~

BACK TO NORMAL?

Arriving home, I had mixed emotions. The house looked the same, even if it did not feel the same. All reminders of the new baby it should have welcomed were gone. I had been looking forward to seeing Claire, as I had not seen her for five days. She looked so cute as she rushed to greet me, in her little cerise dress with white spots and big white collar. As I hugged her I felt so much love for her, yet at the same time I felt so flat and empty. And then I felt guilty for feeling empty when I had such a gorgeous little girl that meant the world to me.

This house still had Stephen and our little Claire. Stephen had been given a week's compassionate leave from work. It was good having this time together. And it was reassuring, in my haze, to share the responsibility of looking after Claire during this first week back at home.

Claire was still a baby herself and, devastated as I was, I had to be there for her. Claire still needed her dinners, have her nappies changed, be played with and cuddled. Things had to carry on as they did before and yet everything had changed. It all felt unreal as I numbly went through the motions of trying to get back to 'normal' life.

Claire was aware that something expected had not happened and that Mummy and Daddy were sad. She also had a sense of loss, although she was not sure what it was. Claire knew that our baby was dead therefore could not come home. She kept drawing dead babies and all kinds of nice dinners she could give them to make them better.

I realised that I would have to explain to her what 'dead' actually meant. But it would have to be in a way that a 21-month old could understand and also not be frightened.

'Dead' could not be 'gone forever' or she would become fearful if I left her for a while. 'Gone to sleep' would make her frightened to go to bed. To say we had 'lost the baby' could make Claire worry that we might lose her too. I could not say that Lisa was 'poorly' or Claire would be scared if she was unwell. So I explained to her that Lisa was not made well enough to live here so she has gone to live with God. Hearing myself vocalise this simple explanation for Claire, in a strange way, also helped me.

My first outing after getting home was to the corner shops. I went on my own, leaving Stephen and Claire at home. Outside the shops, neighbours approached me excitedly. 'Have you had the baby? What did you have?'

I knew I would have to face these questions sometime, but how would I answer them? How could I return their well-meant enquiries with my awful news? I was already aware that it could make others feel uncomfortable. 'I had a little girl' I told them, cautiously. 'Oh congratulations! Where is she then?' So I had to tell them that she had died.

I found that many acquaintances and even some friends were uncomfortable when they saw me. Initially they avoided me, even crossing the road when they saw me, or they avoided any mention of what had happened. I had been warned, though, that they might react like this.

I felt awkward returning to the mother and toddler group with just Claire. I was not taking the new baby I had hoped to bring and others had expected to see. Again I had to tell others the news, to which they clearly did not know how to respond. As I was aware it was my news that made them feel uncomfortable, I found myself reassuring them that I was now alright.

However, I found that many friends really tried to be there for me. If anything, it was almost too much. Unless I went out, somebody called round in the morning and someone else would visit in the afternoon. This went on for weeks. We mostly talked about everyday things, while the children played. I was offered some well-meant comments as attempts to make me feel better. I was told that time would heal. Would it? Time goes on, yes, and life has to carry on but it could never be the same. I was reminded that at least I still had Claire.

Gorgeous as she was, it did not help, as I should also have had Lisa.

I could not talk about how I was feeling inside, because I felt I had been catapulted by the tragedy to a different place and had left my friends far behind. They had not lost a child. They had never held their child in their arms and then felt the anguish of losing it. How could they possibly understand how I felt? I was not sure I really knew myself, though I was certain that I had never ever felt so wrecked.

Although I appreciated their concern and their company, I literally had no space to grieve. There were times I badly needed to cry but I did not want to cry in front of them and make them feel uncomfortable.

I did not want to cry in front of my parents either. I was aware that for them it was probably like a double bereavement. They had lost their grandchild and it would have hurt them even more to see me, their daughter, hurting so much.

I also did not want Claire to see me crying. I was her Mum and she deserved better than that. It was not her fault that I felt so devastated and I did not want her to suffer because of it. So I held back my tears until the evening, when she had gone to bed and Stephen was home from work.

It was hard holding back the tears until I had space to cry and I found that this caused me physical discomfort. I felt pain and tightness in my chest and hollowness in my stomach. I was over-sensitive to external stimuli, especially noise. The sun, which I normally love, just seemed to magnify my despair when it shone. I lacked energy and felt weak, yet I was also restless.

My stomach was baggy from the pregnancy. It looked like a balloon that had been blown up and then not quite deflated. Then there was the wound where I had been opened up to remove the baby. And it had all been for nothing. I was in a strange mixed state of disbelief and yearning for my baby. I felt that Lisa had been cruelly cheated. According to the rhyme, Thursday's child had far to go, but Lisa had lost all chance of 'going' anywhere.

Seeing other new babies surprisingly did not upset me, but seeing a new baby and a toddler in a double buggy really got to me. I spent the evenings looking through the adverts of the local newspaper for double buggies like the one we would have got for Claire and Lisa. (I later learnt that this kind of 'searching' is very normal in bereavement). I knew this was pointless and it made me feel even worse. I found grieving was too painful. I decided I would have to curtail it, try and put it behind me and start to bounce back.

~ *Chapter 6* ~

BOUNCING BACK

One thing I found very therapeutic was to put together a special album as a memory to Lisa. I bought a photo album, selecting one that was grey with pink diagonal stripes because it looked both appropriate and feminine. I collected everything I could about her short life to put in this album - her birth certificate, the photos we had of her (taken by the hospital), her hospital name bracelets and cot card and my pregnancy record card that chronicled her pre-natal development. I also included a photo of what would have been her room and photos of the flowers that I had received. Stephen took me to see where Lisa had been buried and I took a photo of her grave, which I also put in the album. Although there was not really a lot I could put in Lisa's album, it became, none-the-less, a precious memento of her life.

I knew that we could never replace Lisa, but I had a deep and desperate need to have another baby, to fill the emptiness and the unmet expectation of having a second child.

We were invited back to the hospital to see the paediatrician and find out the results of Lisa's post mortem. To get to his room, we were led through the Special Care Baby Unit. It was hard seeing all the tiny babies there. Some of them were attached to machines and monitors. I felt a huge pang, wishing that Lisa could have been there among them - still fighting, still surviving.

We found out that she had heart problems and her lungs had not fully developed. Her heart condition was operable but her lungs were not mature enough to undergo surgery. I expressed my distress about switching off the machine without giving her a chance. Could she not have been kept on it longer so that her lungs could have developed more, and then she could have had the heart operation she needed? We were told that the chances of success were not that good. I was stunned. I was left with the sense that she did then, in fact, have a chance, small as it was.

We were also informed that Lisa's problems were genetic and genetic counselling was arranged. Here we found out that any future baby had a one in four chance of also having these problems. This seemed high. It would now not be so simple to try for another baby. However it also meant that we had a three in four chance of a future baby being all right. This felt more positive and I clung to that.

We were offered various different opinions as to how long it was best to wait after having just had a baby, before we should try again. My own

GP advised me to wait nine months as it takes as long to recover from a pregnancy as the pregnancy itself. The doctor who gave me my six weeks postnatal check up insisted I wait at least twelve months for the caesarean to fully heal internally before I become pregnant again. It was hard to hear this when I wanted another baby now, never mind having to wait to even get pregnant. Yet I knew I had to give the future baby the best chance it could have, especially after what had happened.

The paediatrician understood this and his opinion was that I would not become pregnant unless my body was ready. He suggested that we wait about four months and then see what nature allowed. This felt comfortable to accept.

We had a week's holiday in Tenerife with Claire, to help us recover emotionally from the loss. The family had clubbed together to pay for it. An added incentive to recover physically was the thought of wearing my bikini just nine weeks after having a baby!

The sand, sea and sun, plus all the alcohol and good food (that we did not have to cook) enabled us to enjoy ourselves again. We played with Claire on the beach. Every day, Claire had a long afternoon sleep, which then allowed us to go for evening walks along the promenade and watch the sun set over the sea.

Just before leaving the hotel to fly home, a

woman asked me if I had enjoyed my holiday. 'Yes thanks', I replied and then, without thinking, I added, 'I feel loads better'.

Naturally she asked if I had been ill. As she was a stranger whom I was not likely to meet again, I told her that I had recently lost a baby and we had taken this holiday to recover. She said how sorry she was and then revealed that she could not have children. 'I thought it was bad enough for me,' she said, 'but it must be so much worse to have had a child and then lose it. At least I will never have the pain of losing a child.'

This intimate exchange with a stranger remained in my mind. And it struck me that things were not in fact worse for me. This poor woman would never have the chance to have a child. I had Claire and I still had the chance of trying for another child. As we boarded the plane, I felt hopeful once again.

Five months after losing Lisa, I found out that I was expecting again. I was both excited and apprehensive at the same time. We wondered whether to tell family and friends our news now or whether to wait. In the end we decided to share it, because this was good news and surely they would all be keen to know. Also, this would be an anxious period, worrying if this time things would be all right. I could not expect people to support me if they did not know.

This pregnancy was monitored closely. I was

offered lots of ultrasound scans and an amnio-centesis. I was concerned that an amniocentesis carried a risk of miscarriage but knew that the chance of our baby having problems was greater. I was also aware that having the amniocentesis meant possibly having to make another awful decision. If the results were not good, could we terminate the pregnancy at around five months and end the life of another baby?

While we waited the four weeks for the results, I did not want to think about it. But the issue of late terminations hit the media. It was every-where – debates on the radio, double page spreads in newspapers detailing the pros and cons and mitigating circumstances. Amniocentesis was mentioned specifically. I was trying to forget about it, but I could not escape it at all. Thankfully, at five months pregnant, we were told that everything was fine.

We also learnt that the new baby was a boy. It did not really matter what the baby was as long as it was OK. But as I thought about it, I felt it was better that the baby was not another girl. It meant that this new baby would be loved for himself and not as a replacement for Lisa. We decided we would call him Simon.

From my excitement, Claire knew we had some good news. We felt reasonably confident to now tell her that she was going to have a baby brother. Some of her little friends had babies and she liked the idea of having one too. Would she be able to have it tomorrow? How could I explain time to a two-and-a-half year old? I did so in terms of seasons. It was now cold, then when it gets warmer blossoms appear on the trees and flowers start to grow. And when the Rambler rose in our garden flowers, then our baby will be born. I just willed the Rambler rose not to flower too early!

We arranged for a headstone to be put on Lisa's grave. The wording had to be just right for this public and lasting acknowledgement of her brief life. We decided on the simple inscription 'Will always be remembered' for the grave of our little girl.

On Lisa's first anniversary, we lit a candle for her. It was a day of mixed emotions - remembering Lisa and also, as I was very pregnant, looking forward to Simon's arrival in just two month's time.

Our attention was also focused on Stephen finding another job. Because of losing Lisa, his work had suffered to the extent that he was 'encouraged' to leave the company. We tried not to allow this second blow to beat us. Stephen was determined to find a new position before the baby was born and when I was 37 weeks pregnant, he had secured another job.

It would necessitate another move to a different town. We found ourselves travelling to look for a new house at 38 weeks, hoping that as the birth was so imminent this would not lead to another motorway labour. However this time Stephen could drive and the baby obligingly waited.

I knew when the baby was due, that he was a little boy, his name would be Simon and that he was likely to have ginger hair. This made the last two weeks of my pregnancy feel like I was waiting on the platform for his train to arrive. And on the due date itself, a ginger-haired Simon arrived on time. As I held Simon in my arms, it was difficult to let myself believe that this time I had a baby I could keep.

~ *Chapter 7* ~

MOVING ON

Three weeks after Simon was born, we moved to a new town. I had wanted to move after losing Lisa and now we were, but this time it was for the right reason. Stephen had a new job. Although I found it was very stressful moving with a toddler and a three-week-old baby (and this was an under-statement!), it was to be a new start for the four of us.

Stephen's parents came up and helped us unpack all our things in the new house. I remember panicking about there not being adequate fencing round the house. I was concerned about Claire being in the garden. If I took my eyes off her for just a minute, to tend to the baby, Claire could escape out to the front and onto the busy road. We had to find someone to erect a fence as soon as possible. Once the fence was in place, I was able to relax.

We settled quickly in the new town. Stephen adjusted to his new job. I found a new mother and toddler group where I met other mothers and made new friends. Within six days of moving, I was invited round with Claire and Simon to somebody's house and I felt I had arrived.

With life now looking good, we decided to try

for another child. We knew we still carried the same one-in-four risk of problems. We had been lucky with Claire and with Simon, which was encouraging. But even though the risk was the same for each baby, having been lucky twice, I felt that maybe we were less likely to be this time. I pushed this thought out of my mind. We were in a new town and having a new start. I forced myself to stay positive as we embarked on another pregnancy.

My medical records were transferred from the previous hospital. At my initial antenatal appointment at the hospital, the consultant came to see me. He spent a long time looking at my notes, reading about my 'history', nodding every now and again.

He then asked me if I had realised that we could have a baby with the same problems as Lisa but not quite as severe. We could have a baby who was very ill but still live. This meant bringing into the world a child who would suffer. I was stunned. We had not realised this awful possibility when we had decided to risk trying for another baby, Simon or this one. And I was now being told here, with a baby already growing inside me.

The hospital monitored me closely, which was reassuring. I had another amniocentesis and, after a nerve-wracking wait, again received the news that things were fine.

Joanne was born 20 months after Simon. But when she was just five days old, we found out that our seemingly healthy baby had heart problems. I felt crushed. By having another baby, had we pushed our luck too far?

We anxiously waited while Joanne had X-rays and all sorts of instruments were attached to her tiny body. Finally we were told that her problems were operable with a high success rate. I was relieved, as Joanne would be getting the chance I wished Lisa could have had. But at the same time I felt sick with worry, as this was my baby who would have to face this surgery.

However, we were told that there was a small chance that things might right themselves as Joanne grew and she would be reassessed when she was six months old. It was a long anxious six months. Yet with each passing month, seeing Joanne thrive, I began to dare myself to be hopeful. And, despite being told there was a small chance, it was our time to be lucky. By the time Joanne was twelve months old she was discharged from the hospital and we were reassured that she could lead a normal life.

We enjoyed the three children and I felt lucky to have them. However, we had initially hoped to have four children. Since losing Lisa, we had lessened our dreams to seeing if we could have just one more child. And when we did, we again felt we would try for one more if we were able to.

However, after a couple of years, we wondered if we would really be pushing our luck too far if we tried just once more. My attitude was that if you do not try then you never gain. I did not want to look back when we were older, wishing that we had.

So once again we tried not to think of the risks. Especially after the initial worries we had with Joanne, we pushed all such thoughts even further from our minds. At first, I did not even want to have the amniocentesis, in an attempt to try and pretend that everything was all right. Stephen wanted the reassurance of having it done and so did I, really. I was jovially told that 'we don't normally give people three amnios, you know'. I was aware of the message behind the words – people with risks do not normally push their luck this much.

At the same time as getting the amniocentesis results, I was going to have an ultrasound scan. Claire, who had now just turned seven, wanted to come with me to see the scan. I was at the stage of pregnancy where a scan gave an optimum view of the baby. She wanted to see it growing inside me and was fascinated to see what an unborn baby looked like.

I realised that this would probably be my last pregnancy and it would be a unique opportunity for Claire to see a baby on a scan. Yet I was also aware that, although I did not want to think about it, there was the possibility that I might not be able to keep the baby. How would Claire then cope, if she had seen it on the scan? But if she did not see the scan and the worst was to happen, it would still be a big loss to her and she would have also missed the opportunity to see it.

So I decided that if I carefully and truthfully explained the situation to Claire, it would be good to let her come and see the baby on the scan.

While a friend looked after Simon and Joanne, I took Claire out of school and she accompanied me to the hospital. She was with me when I was told that the amniocentesis results were good and we both had a glimpse of our future baby.

Then at last, a few days before Christmas, John was born, safe and healthy.

Claire was intrigued with the new baby, a brand new little person. Simon, who was now four and a bundle of energy, was especially thrilled to have a little brother. Joanne, at two and a half, just picked up and joined in the general joy and relief.

We now had the family that we had hardly dared hoped we would have.

~ *Chapter 8* ~

IT WOULDN'T LIE QUIET

One year after John was born, we moved to another city.

Life was busy and hectic but I felt proud and really fortunate whenever I mentioned that I have four children. And I was amused by the many reactions that I 'must be mad'.

However, I occasionally felt a pang saying that I have four children. It was as if I was denying Lisa's brief existence. I had never kept it a secret, but it was not something I could casually mention in conversation.

When I did tell other people about her, they often responded with something totally inappropriate or they were clearly uncomfortable. Again I found myself trying to make them feel better and I wondered whether I had been unwise to tell them.

As it approached what would have been Lisa's tenth birthday, I began to feel a resurgence of sadness. We had lit a candle every year on her birthday in memory of our little girl, but this time it felt different. I have always considered a 'double figure' birthday as a landmark, yet there could be no celebration. I looked at other ten year old girls and wondered if Lisa would have been anything like them.

Stephen was surprised when I told him how I felt. He thought that, like him, I had dealt with the loss and put it behind me. I realised that I could not have dealt with it properly. He had put all his sadness and pain behind him and was not keen to reopen it again. I could understand this.

I have a close friend called Susan. She'd had the courage to share her innermost feelings with me. I had always been a very open person, able to talk about any topic at all, but I realised that apart from Stephen I had never told anyone about my feelings. To do so would be peeling off my protective layers and leaving me vulnerable. But I knew I could be vulnerable with Susan.

As I began to share with Susan how I felt, it became clear just how sad I still was about losing Lisa and how tormented I felt about switching off her life support machine. I had put it all 'under the carpet' when the pain of grief had got too much and after a while it just wouldn't lie quiet.

I realised that I would have to allow myself the natural time to grieve, even though it was now ten years on. This time, I could not bypass it or rush it, but had to see it through. I remembered the scar Dan had talked about. It was no use covering up an unhealed scar as it would still be there. But if I allowed it to heal properly, maybe I could carry Lisa with me more comfortably.

I felt that I needed to visit Lisa's grave. We had

not been for over nine years, since it was in a different town and an effort to get to. Also as I had been trying to put the past behind me, I had not felt the need to go. But now I had a real need and I felt that to go on the tenth anniversary of her funeral would be perfect.

I wanted to go with just Stephen, as I wanted this trip to be healing for me. My Mum agreed to look after the children. We could always take them to the grave at a later date.

On the day that would have been Lisa's tenth birthday, it was unseasonably warm. While the three older children were at school and John was at play-school, I had a quiet time looking at the album I had made for Lisa. And I thought about the day ten years ago, when she had been born and then died. I recognised that this birthday was a landmark for both Lisa and myself. It was ten years on, an important anniversary for me and still a 'double figure' birthday for her.

I made a birthday cake to share with Stephen and the children in the evening. I lit a candle for her. The children were aware that this was Lisa's birthday and they each understood it in their own way.

The day of our trip to Lisa's grave was also a warm spring day. We set off in time to be at the graveside for the exact time of her funeral ten years earlier. Then in my own manner, I could create a way of saying goodbye to Lisa.

Stephen was driving and I navigated. When we were nearly there, we got to a roundabout off the motorway. I told Stephen that we needed the third exit to join the next motorway. But seeing a signpost, Stephen took the second exit instead. I complained in horror that we had gone wrong. Now we would be late and I would not be at the grave at the time I had really wanted to be.

As he could not turn round, I consulted the map to find out how we could now get there. And to my amazement, it meant that at the next junction we would join the route that the original funeral had taken. We arrived at Lisa's grave with just one minute to go.

Not only were we there on the tenth anniversary and at the exact time of her funeral, we had by accident (or was it fate?) also taken the same route.

At the grave, we put down some flowers that we had brought. I was relieved to see that the grave and headstone were in good condition. I sat for a while with my eyes shut and quietly spoke to Lisa. I told her the things that I wished I had been awake enough to say as I was holding her before she died. It felt good to be able to say this to her. I needed to be here at the grave to do it.

I took some photos of the grave with the flowers and Stephen took some photos of me at the grave. I then selected five white pebbles from the site of the grave to take home. One was for me, to be a concrete memento of our visit, to look at or hold in my hand if I needed to. The other four were to give to the children when they are older. I took one small flower to take home to press and put in Lisa's album. (It did not actually work but I had the photos of the flowers, which I put in her album.)

When we were ready to leave, I felt I had not just said 'goodbye' but 'hello' as well. This was also something that I had not had the chance to say to her. It was a welcome, though not to the world but to me.

After the visit, the weight of loss seemed lightened and I felt I was 'carrying' Lisa with me now. However, the guilt of having agreed to switch off her life support machine was slowly creeping in.

I shared this with a few close friends. They had mostly responded in a similar way, saying that Lisa would have probably been a very sick child and that we had been, or Lisa had been, spared this.

I realised that these reassurances were logically right and I managed to push my guilt aside. But not for long, because feelings do not go away just because other people deny them or because they do not follow logic. The platitudes, though well meant, had just allowed me to avoid looking at my uncomfortable feelings, which were still there.

External factors, such as poignant film scenes or

evocative songs or tragic events in the news, were now touching something deep inside me.

My friend Susan did not try and get me away from how I felt, for my sake or hers. She wondered, however, whether this was something that maybe I would never come to terms with.

I recognised that she could be right. However there was something within me that compelled me to try and become more comfortable and I sought counselling. I would do my best to try and come to terms with what I had done.

~ *Chapter 9* ~

LOOKING INWARDS

This is the chapter that I found hardest to write. It was hard to share in print the intensely personal area of facing all my feelings through counselling. Yet, I recognised that there would be a huge gap if I skipped over this. There would also be a lost opportunity of maybe helping others if I did not share my own journey of recovery.

I was both nervous and hopeful at the prospect of counselling. I was nervous of having to tell, and probably show, a complete stranger how I felt. But I was also hoping that this would lead to me feeling better.

I started to tell the counsellor the whole story of losing my child, but for some reason I felt inhibited from really telling her about the pain of it all.

I tried to voice my feelings about the hospital not allowing me more time to 'come to', before asking my permission to switch off Lisa's life support machine. But she totally blocked this. She said that it was all 'if only' talk, not what actually happened and that focusing on it was destructive. She told me that I *had* made this decision and we needed to work with that.

However, I felt I could not 'work' without going over all this. (I later learnt that 'if only' feelings are often a big part of bereavement.) I felt I was fighting to get the counsellor to hear me. It was as if she was denying me my feelings. I knew that counselling should be about exploring feelings and wondered if maybe this counsellor was not right for me.

In fact, her insistence that it was I who had decided to switch off the machine only made me feel worse about what I had done. I needed to find another counsellor.

It was hard to start again and retell my story. But the new counsellor, Jackie, was very genuine and not ashamed to show that she was moved by what I told her. She allowed me to talk about how it was untimely and in the 'wrong order' to lose a child, and to really express the sadness I felt inside.

She was totally accepting of all the 'if only' feelings and allowed me to go over and over the anguish I felt about switching off the machine. At the core of this anguish was my small drowsy voice saying 'no', being squashed by their big voice saying it should be turned off and implying that I would otherwise be denying Lisa her dignity.

Looking at it now, this felt like emotional blackmail. Yet, even though I was still drowsy, why had I not managed to rise above it? I had not saved her. By agreeing to switch her off, I felt I had killed my little girl.

Jackie had allowed me to voice the unspeakable, without trying to counter it or 'move' me somewhere else. I pictured Lisa in my arms, wrapped in the blanket, and it hurt even more.

Jackie was angry on my behalf, for having to make such an awful and irreversible decision when not in a fit state to. And then for having not been heard. 'Bastards', she said softly. I slowly realised that the hospital had abused my right as a mother and my right to make an informed choice about switching off Lisa's machine. I had been powerless and then robbed of the chance to save my child. The deep disappointment I felt in myself shifted to anger towards the doctors.

It was hard for me to initially own this anger, as I had not been able to see beyond the feelings of guilt. I then realised that I had suppressed the anger for over ten years because of this guilt and devastating sadness. Yet, I recognised that to feel this anger would be healing and could spur me on to resolve things.

Despite feeling anger towards the doctors, I somehow still needed Lisa's forgiveness for what had happened - which of course was not possible. Jackie felt that this was putting the responsibility of my feeling better onto Lisa. But I felt it was not my place to forgive myself and wondered how I could move on.

Jackie helped me to realise that if I have hurt someone, then I am only responsible for how I feel and what I subsequently do. After I have apologised and made amends if I wish to, it is up to the other person to forgive me if and when they are ready and choose to. But I can decide when I feel sorry enough to let it go and forgive myself. This is not looking for answers from outside, which can falter or be taken back, but reclaiming some power over myself.

I felt I had certainly suffered enough. At an earlier stage of my counselling, I had got a copy made of Lisa's photograph from her album and put it up on the wall. I wanted to acknowledge that she was still a part of us, to give the children a tangible way of acknowledging their sister, and for people to see and acknowledge our other child.

Also, as her grave was not nearby, I had created my own special focus for her. On my way to one of my previous counselling sessions, for some reason I had taken a different route and passed a church with a cemetery. It was sunny and I stopped to admire the flowers on the graves. They looked beautiful in the sun and I felt a pang inside. Lisa's grave was so far away and I could hardly ever place flowers there. I realised that I needed some other special focus for her.

I talked to Jackie about it. I felt that a little

glass box of stones would be meaningful, if I selected the right stones. It would be Lisa's box. I knew one of the stones would be the little white pebble that I had taken from her grave, and another would be the gemstone associated with her zodiac birth-sign. I added a clear quartz stone with a diagonal inclusion in it, which looked like an aerial that was a connection to Lisa.

I felt I needed one more stone and with nothing specific in mind and open to choosing it intuitively, I picked out an orange carnelian. I think the colour attracted me as it matched Lisa's hair. When I held it to the light, I saw an inclusion that looked like the symbol of her birth-sign. It was perfect. It was as if Lisa had chosen it through me. I felt I had made amends the best way that I could.

I was now ready to forgive myself. Voicing this to Jackie made it more concrete. It felt as if the heaviness had lifted, like held-back balloons that had finally been set free...

I was ready to finish counselling. It had been a very special relationship. I had received so much from Jackie. She said that she had also gained so much from me, that she had felt privileged to witness my courage in facing my pain and coming through it.

The pain was not sorted and sealed away, but now more comfortable. I am sure I will always feel a deep sadness that could be stirred unexpectedly at any time. But I feel that is how it should be. At such times I find it good when I listen to music, picking songs that 'empathise' with how I feel. I almost like this sadness, because it feels as if I am carrying Lisa with me.

~ *Chapter 10* ~

STIRRING PACIFIED WATERS

As life carried on, I found a place within me where I could hold my thoughts and feelings about Lisa and what had happened. In quieter moments I sometimes visited this place. I had found some inner comfort and peace.

All the children were now at school. Stephen's work was going well and I had a job that I found stimulating and I could fit round school hours. Life was good.

The New Millennium was welcomed with much excitement and celebration. Yet with this new era of better times, came the rumbling of medical atrocities.

First at Alder Hey Hospital in Liverpool, the nation learned that thousands of organs from dead children and babies had been retained. Parents had unknowingly buried their children with parts of them missing. By January 2001 it emerged that this scandal was not just confined to Alder Hey. Organs were held at many hospitals throughout the country.

A sense of unease was slowly creeping over me. Could they also have taken something from Lisa? Had we buried her intact? Or was something of hers in a jar or drawer in some hospital pathology department? After the enormous trauma we had been through and finally put behind us, could this horror also be happening to us?

Although I was reluctant to reawaken the pain, I could not leave myself with the doubts and fears I now had. Feeling like I was taking a huge step back towards darker times, I nervously picked up the telephone and phoned the hospital.

I was connected to a help line. A recorded message acknowledged my call. I had come through to the hospital help line and they were handling inquiries about organs that may have been retained after post mortem examinations. I took a deep breath as a real person then came on the other end of the line and asked how she could help.

Once again I had to retell my story, this time to an unknown and unseen person on the phone. I hesitated as I spoke. I began to feel distressed but I could not discern how my words were impacting on this other person.

The female voice gently prompted me for relevant details, such as the date and place Lisa died. She used Lisa's name throughout the conversation, which felt strangely warming. But it was a sharp acknowledgement of both Lisa's existence and her death. It was a stirring up of pacified waters and the start of a long six months wait for answers.

I was told that rigid procedures had been introduced. These were to ensure that families did not suffer the added trauma of discovering piecemeal about retained organs, with the possible ordeal of multiple burials. Hospitals involved had to catalogue all stored organs, with multiple checks, and enter their 'stock taking' onto a database. Only after receiving a government go ahead, could hospitals actually begin their search for the information that we were anxiously awaiting.

As the weeks turned into months, the waiting became unbearable. All I wanted was an answer: did they have any of our child's organs or not? Would we have to go through the ordeal of a second burial? I was in turmoil. One emotion merged into another as I swung between acute distress, extreme anger, nausea, disbelief and agitation. I was desperate for an answer.

Outside my turbulent world, this had also become a media scandal. When I did speak about the hell I was going through, many people reacted with shock. This atrocity was happening to someone they knew. I felt as if there was a public interest in my private torment.

One evening towards the end of April, Stephen and I were watching the Ten O'clock News. A reporter announced the imminent release of information from hospitals about retained organs. It would be the end of the agony for those families caught up in this ordeal. We sat there speechless. How come we were hearing this on the News? Why could the hospital not have told us personally? Or had the media got hold of this and leaked it out to the nation?

The reporter went on to say that for each of these families, decisions now had to be made: whether to have a second burial, ask the hospital to dispose of the organs respectfully, or to donate them to research. We were watching some stranger talking about us! I was shocked and indignant. How could this person assume to know what we were feeling or thinking? Or how we would respond to information we were about to get?

More weeks passed and still no answer came. I phoned the help line. The media report of imminent answers was in fact just the government go ahead for hospitals to start the search. It would be another few weeks before they could tell me anything. I thought the finishing line had finally been in sight, but now it had moved somewhere further away. I felt so frustrated and let down.

The woman on the phone asked if I had access to any emotional support. I realised this was something I clearly needed. The hospital agreed to fund some counselling.

I decided to contact Jackie, who had helped me so much before, hoping she would be able and willing to see me soon. Jackie was really sorry to hear about what was happening and said she would be pleased to work with me again.

It was mid July when a formal-looking white envelope dropped through our letterbox. Unsuspectingly, I opened it and from the headed paper I could see that it was a letter from the hospital. In an instant, I felt as if the contents of my stomach lurched upwards, leaving a huge gaping void where they used to be. Was this, at last, the information I had been waiting for? Nervously, I began to read the printed letter in my hands.

It started with the conventional 'further to your enquiry' and an apology for the delayed reply. It went on to relate details that they had already told me over the phone. 'It was routine practice...' the letter continued. Then came the words that confirmed my worst fear. Part of Lisa's liver had been retained. And worse still, due to some subsequent testing of the tissue, it had all been destroyed. Lisa was lying in her grave with part of her missing and now we had no chance at all of making her whole again.

The letter ended with an expression of regret for any distress this matter may have caused.

I was stunned. I could hardly take in what I

had just read. Yet my body reacted immediately. My stomach heaved and tears were rolling down my cheeks. My brain felt disconnected, whilst the rest of me was totally gutted. In just a few minutes my whole sense of reality had been blown apart and the bottom of the once pacified waters had completely dropped away.

~ *Chapter 11* ~

THE NIGHTMARE CONTINUES

Nothing around me felt solid. I expected to free fall. But I didn't. Instead it seemed as if I was left suspended. Suspended somewhere above the familiar reality of my everyday world. Near, but not quite able to touch or engage with it.

Seeing Jackie enabled me to find a kind of anchor. With her I was able to give some shape and form to all the intense emotions that were flooding through me. I had a place where I could start to untangle the turmoil within and express feelings that were so often beyond words.

I felt deeply wounded, angry and very betrayed. When Lisa's life support machine was switched off, they had told us it was better to let her die with dignity. And now we have found out that they have not allowed her to rest with dignity. It was a huge betrayal of trust.

We were never asked if they could have her liver - not that I could even begin to think how we would have responded at the time. Nor were we informed afterwards of what they had done. They had stolen it. And for all these years, we never knew.

How could a medical institution, of all places,

steal parts from a dead person? Steal from a defenceless dead child? How low could they sink? It was the most deep and immoral violation, an injustice beyond depravity and belief.

When my Mum took Lisa to the hospital morgue, I thought she would be safe there. Instead, she was left to await her fate. She had not even been safe in death.

For quite some time, I had disturbed sleep and horrific nightmares. I saw shelves and shelves of impersonal jars, containing dismembered body parts. Any one of them could have been Lisa's. One night I dreamed that we were lining Lisa's grave with cement to try and protect her, so that nobody could ever get to her now.

I could not comprehend the horror of what they had done to Lisa after she left the safety of my arms. With Jackie, I felt I could risk venturing into this dark and gruesome place, to try and get my head round it.

I visualised her mutilated, cut and stitched up little body. I had an image of my beautiful child, in a cold bleak room with a stone floor, lying naked and vulnerable on a wooden table. Standing over her was a cold, faceless person, wielding a cold and steely knife.

What kind of person could possibly do this? Could he have his own children, or grandchildren, that he loved and cared for? Yet he could turn into the savage butcher who violated my child?

Did this butcher have any sensitivity as he hacked Lisa's little body, now that the flame of life had gone out of it? Was he touched at all by the fact that her flame did burn for a short while, that she was our child and precious to us? Or was she just a cold slab of meat, an object containing organs that he could plunder?

It is suitably ironic that the word 'doctor' can also mean to botch, alter, change, disguise, falsify, pervert and tamper with - all with unethical and deceptive connotations. Through the hands of a doctor, we had been deceived and robbed.

Lisa had been robbed of her life and then of her liver and her dignity. We had been robbed of a chance to return the liver to her and, in so doing, find some kind of completion.

Anger was firing up inside me. But it had no outlet. At whom could I lash out and scream? The fury seemed trapped within me and the pain felt unbearable. I needed to vent my anger to the appropriate people, even though I did not know who they were. I could do this by writing a letter. A letter that I would not actually send, but could write and let rip without censure or concern.

I wrote one letter to the pathologist and another to the doctor who made us switch off Lisa's life support machine. I had quite a few attempts until the wording felt exactly right – emphatic, strong and unrestrained.

Through writing the letters I tapped into the

anger and gave it voice and release. This was reinforced by reading them out loud to Stephen and also to Jackie at my next session.

Initially I was disturbed by the intensity of my anger, but at the same time it felt appropriate and strengthening. I found I had a power in my anger and in my not forgiving - or not until such a time as I feel ready.

With Stephen, I then held a ceremony to burn the letters. It was a very symbolic ritual. I was burning demons at the stake. And also, although not yet forgiving, I was letting go of the intensity of feelings so that I could move on. As each letter charred and smouldered, I said 'I am letting go of you and the pain you have caused'. And watching the smoke rising from the ashes, I already felt lighter and free.

I have the rest of my life ahead of me and I want to live it as fully as I can.

~ *Chapter 12* ~

A Sacred Flame

I have now come to terms with my loss and for my part in switching off Lisa's life support machine. However, I am not yet ready to forgive the hospital for the way they handled it.

I feel that I should have been given more time to 'come to' before having to make the decision. They should have waited until I was alert enough to discuss it with the doctors. Then, maybe Lisa would still be here. Maybe she would not. But then I could have made an informed decision to turn off the machine. Painful as this would have been, to me this would be easier to live with than having been powerless to prevent it being turned off and ending Lisa's life.

Also, I am not yet ready to forgive the despicable violation of Lisa's body and her dignity.

However, I have received a letter from the hospital, in which they acknowledge all the pain that this has caused, admit responsibility and give an unreserved apology.

This is an extract from the letter:

"I know that the last few months must have been very difficult for you, constantly being reminded of the grief and pain you suffered all those years ago when Lisa died. However, I hope you also know that there is widespread recognition across the NHS that the way we did things in the past was not always the best way, but most things were done with the best intentions, and we have learned. You will be glad to know that we have changed the way we deal with loss and bereavement in many ways and although it won't help you, those who suffer the same loss will not have the same experience as you did…

… I know that you have found this difficult to deal with and there is little more we can say to you that will help. Those of us who have been working with all the families and parents who have contacted us, have found it distressing and difficult. We understand your concern but are powerless to give you the complete closure you would like. I can only apologise on behalf of the NHS for the way in which this whole issue has brought back to you the pain of losing Lisa."

This acknowledgement and apology from the hospital has helped to lessen my anguish that they had got away with it.

I know that nothing can ever undo what has happened or recompense our loss and our suffering. Yet I wanted acknowledgement of Lisa's life, the pain and the atrocious injustice inflicted upon us. That was one of the reasons for writing this story.

I also hope that through writing my story, I may give comfort to others who have lost a child and that lessons will be learnt.

As for me, I feel happy and lucky to now have four lovely children. Naturally, I do still have times when I wish Lisa could be with us too, but I know hers could only be a fleeting visit.

I feel that Lisa's life was like a candle. Her flame only burned for a short while. It had been a wobbly, struggling flame that had been snuffed out prematurely, before it had the chance to run its natural course. Before it had the chance to burn for long, allowing its wax to melt and transform its shape over time. We never saw its full potential. The sacred flame of life had been extinguished. And its sanctity had been violated. But I realise now, that although a physical part of Lisa is missing, her spirit endures.

My journey through grief involved looking deep within myself and I have found so much that could otherwise have remained hidden. In times of limbo and stillness there was a fertile void, from where understanding and awareness often emerged.

I have also recognised that it is good to feel all my emotions – happiness, sadness, anger, calm, excitement, apprehension, hope and despair – because to feel is to be really alive. To only feel some things is to only be half-alive and I deserve better than that. I now feel fully alive and this is the treasure that I have found from the wreckage of pain.

As I carry this treasure within myself, a part of

Lisa remains with me.

If this story helps or touches another human soul, then the spirit of Lisa's flame will continue to glow.

A candle burns
Then its flame is gone,
Yet through our souls
Does the gift live on...

OTHER BOOKS FROM PENNINE PENS

THE CURIOUS CASE OF DR MANN by Trevor Millum

A VIEW FROM THE BRIDGE - John Morrison
BACK TO THE BRIDGE - John Morrison
A BRIDGE TOO FAR - John Morrison

BERRINGDEN BROW by Jill Robinson
     40-something woman's search for romance

ANIMAL ANTICS
     a collection of children's poems by Debjani Chatterjee.
THE REDLIT BOYS - a collection of poems by William Bedford
EMAIL FROM THE PROVINCES
     Poems by Simon Fletcher
NANNY KNOWS BEST - ebook novel from Simon Fletcher
A LITTLE BRIDGE, a collection of poems by Debjani Chatterjee,
Basir Kazmi and Simon Fletcher. These three talented Northern
poets have collaborated in a collection of poems which reflects
the connections between the cultures of Britain and the Indian
sub-continent.
The Occasions of Love
     Love poems by Simon Fletcher
THE CHESS BOARD, a play by Basir Kazmi

ME, MICK AND M31 by Andrew Bibby
     Children's environmental mystery

CYCLING IN SEARCH OF THE CATHARS by Chris Ratcliffe and
Elaine Connell - CD-rom and online ebook versions only of
book available

SYLVIA PLATH: KILLING THE ANGEL IN THE HOUSE (2nd edition)
by Elaine Connell, A very readable introduction to the works of
this great poet. Elaine Connell also maintains the **Sylvia Plath
Forum** - www.sylviaplathforum.com

More details of Pennine Pens publications and web design at

www.penninepens.co.uk